# Levers

written by Mandy Suhr
and illustrated by Mike Gordon

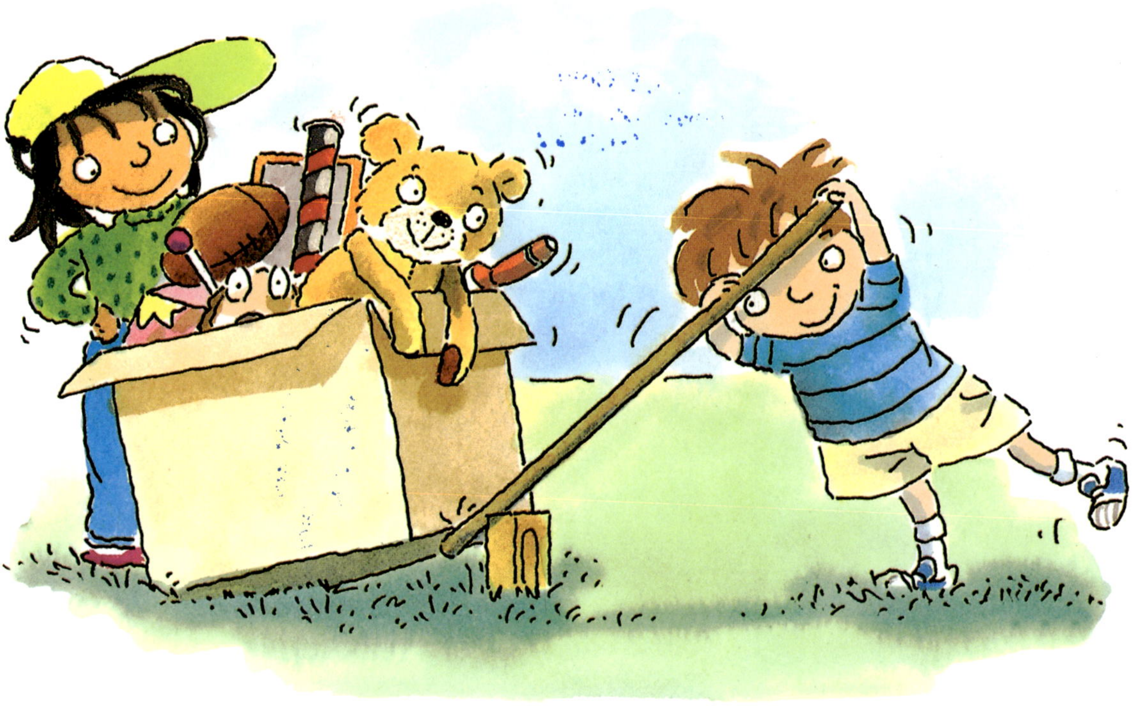

WAYLAND

First published in Great Britain in 1996
by Wayland (Publishers) Ltd
This edition printed in 2001 by Hodder Wayland

This revised edition published in 2009 by Wayland,
338 Euston Road, London NW1 3BH

Wayland Australia,
Level 17/207 Kent Street, Sydney, NSW 2000

Copyright © Wayland 1996

British Library Cataloguing in Publication Data
Suhr, Mandy.
　Levers. -- (Simple technology)
　1. Levers--Juvenile literature.
　I. Title II. Series
　621.8'11-dc22

ISBN 978-0-7502-5954-5

Printed in China

Wayland is a division of Hachette Children's Books, an Hachette UK Company
www.hachette.co.uk

Contents

What is a lever?	4
Forces	6
The first levers	8
Using levers	10
Different parts	12
Look around	14
A seesaw	16
Experiment with levers	18
More levers	20
Everyday levers	22
Your body	24
Different levers	26
Glossary	28
Notes for adults	29
Further information	30
Index	32

We use machines everyday to help us to do all sorts of things. Some machines are big and complicated.

Some are very simple.

A lever is probably one of the simplest machines there is.

A lever can make moving something easier. This is because it can turn a small force into a bigger force. A force is the energy that makes something move. Pushing and pulling are both forces.

Take a ball of plasticine in your hands. Push and pull it into different shapes.

The force, or pushing and pulling, of your fingers makes the plasticine move.

Levers were probably first used by Stone Age people. They may have moved heavy rocks by using branches as levers.

Try this for yourself. Find a strong stick and put one end under a heavy cardboard box. Next, push a smaller object under the stick (for the stick to rest on).

Press down on the top end of the stick. Can you see how the bottom end is forced up, making the box move?

A lever has three parts.

The force arm. This is the part of the lever which is forced up or down.

The load arm. This is the part of the lever which moves the load.

The fulcrum. This is the part where the lever turns, moves, or balances.

You probably use lots of levers.

At your desk....

...in the garden

...around the house

...and in the garage.

A lever can be very useful for a burglar!

When you go to the park
you may even sit on a lever!

A seesaw is a lever. When you sit on one end, your weight acts as a force. It pushes your end down and the other end up.
Two children of about the same weight can move the ends of a seesaw up and down!

Make a seesaw

Rest a long plank of wood on a brick. (Make sure the brick is in the middle.) The place where the brick rests on the plank is the fulcrum.

What happens if two children sit on one end of the seesaw lever?

Move the brick towards the end of the seesaw with the heavier weight. What happens now?

A light weight can lift a heavy weight if the heavy weight is nearest to the fulcrum.

Levers come in all sorts of useful shapes and sizes.

A wheelbarrow is a lever. The wheel acts as the fulcrum. When you pull up the handles, this small force can lift a heavy load.

A nutcracker is also a lever. The fulcrum is where the two arms join at one end. When you push the two arms together, this small force turns into a greater force nearer to the fulcrum. This crushes the nut.

A pair of tongs is a slightly different lever. You squeeze the tongs, or apply a force in the middle. This allows the tongs to hold an object in place.

Some parts of your body are levers. Your arms are levers which can lift heavy weights.

Your muscles apply a force which moves the bones in your arms up and down. Your elbow joint acts as a fulcrum.

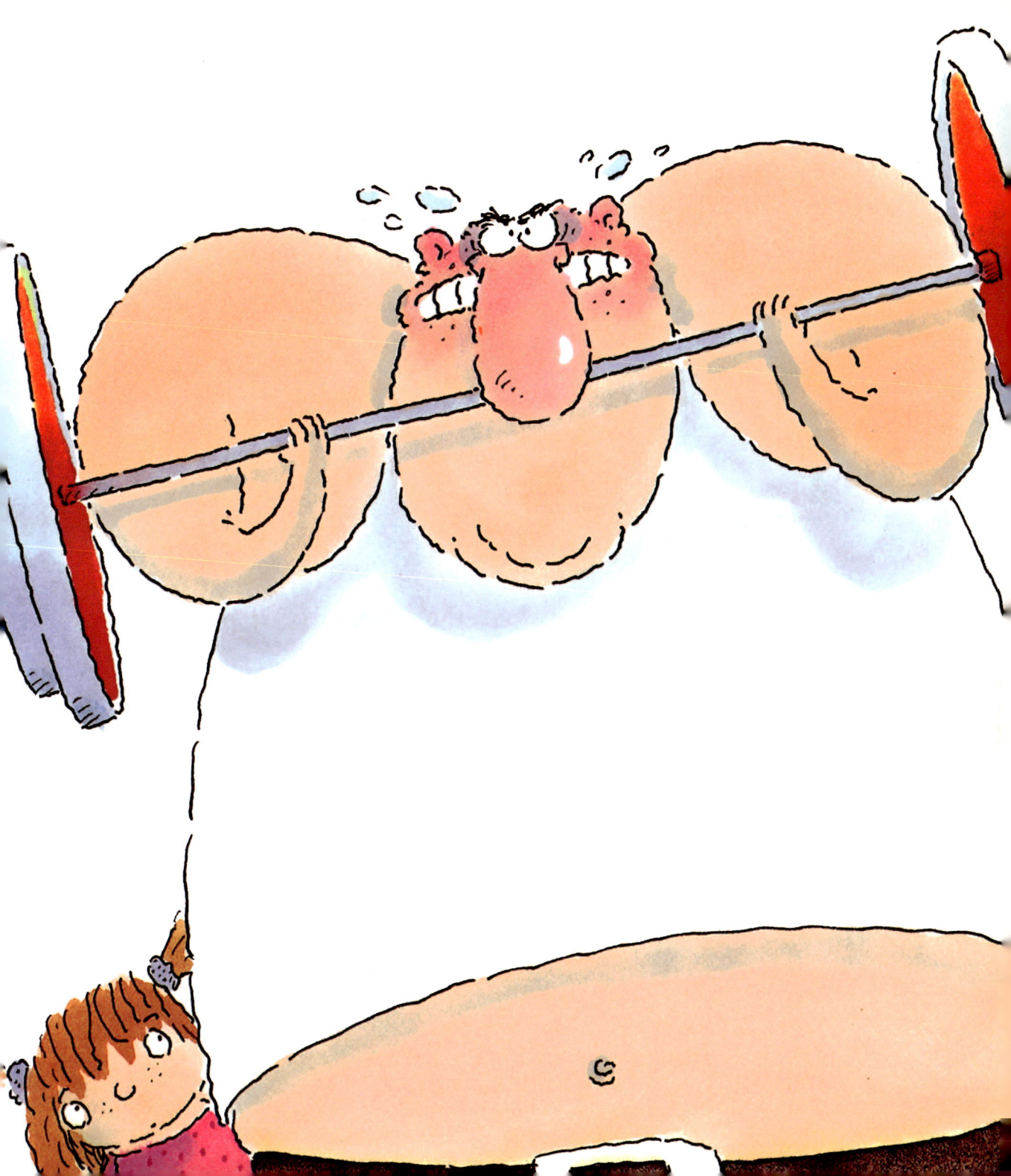

Make a snappy crocodile puppet with a lever jaw

Some levers don't lift weights - they just move things up and down.

You will need:
- Stiff card • 1 piece of wooden dowling
- 2 brass split pins • Sticky tape

1. Cut out a crocodile shape. Separate the jaw piece, and cut a separate strip of card.

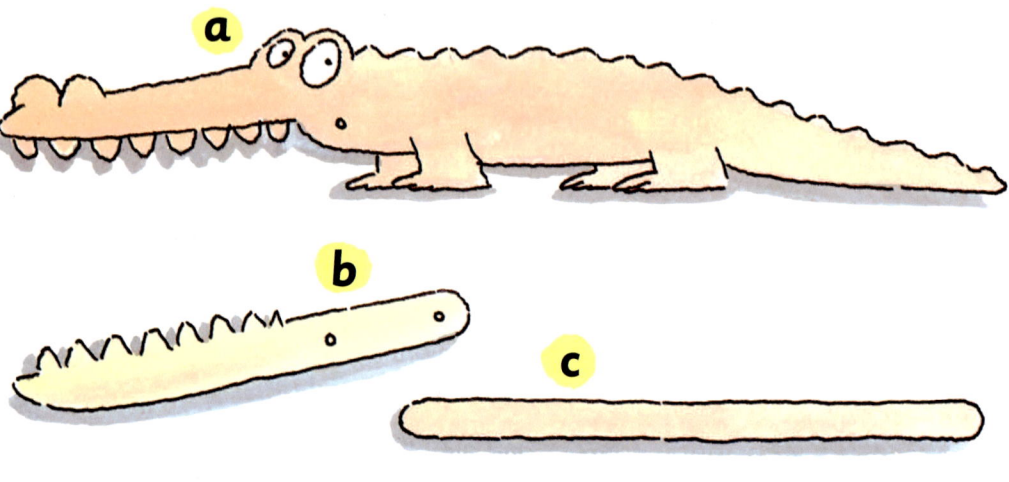

2. Join the jaw piece and card strip with a split pin.

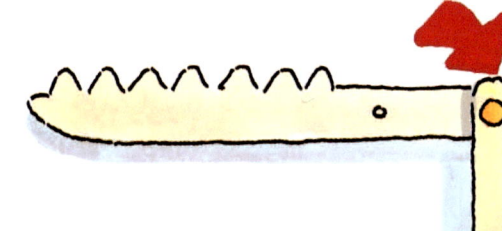

3. Join the jaw piece to the body of your crocodile with the other split pin.

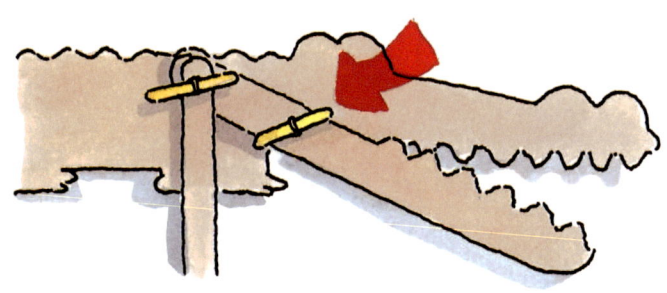

4. Attach the wooden dowling with sticky tape, to use as a handle.

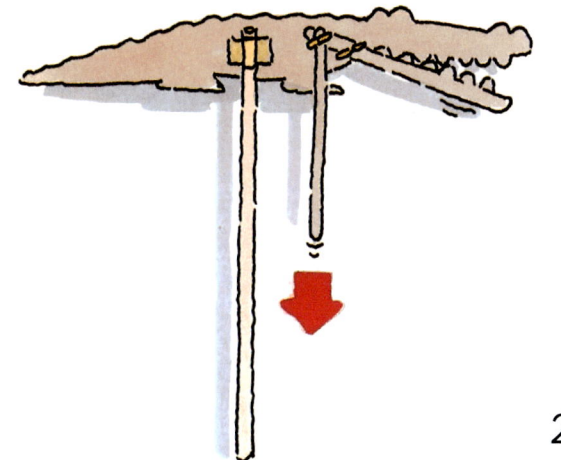

5. Pull the card strip to make the crocodile's jaws snap!

Glossary

Energy — The power to do work.
Force — A push or pull on an object.
Force arm — The part of the lever to which the force is applied.
Fulcrum — The point on which a lever balances or turns.
Load — The weight of the object that is to be moved by the lever.
Load arm — The part of a lever which moves the load.
Machine — A device to make work easier.

Notes for adults

Simple Technology is a series of elementary books designed to introduce children to the everyday machines which make all of our lives easier, and the basic principles behind them.

For millions of years people have been inventing and using machines to make work easier. These machines have been constantly modified and redesigned over the years to make them more sophisticated and more successful at their task. This is really what technology is all about. It is the process of applying knowledge to make work easier.

In these books, children are encouraged to explore the early inspirations for machines, and the process of modification that has brought them forward in their current state, and in doing so, come to an understanding of the design process.

The simple text and humorous illustrations give a clear explanation of how these machines actually work, and experiments and activities give suggestions for further practical exploration.

Suggestions for further activities

* Make a collection of levers and encourage children to test them out.

* Explore the principle of force, including different ways of creating a force.

* To further examine how a lever can multiply a force, encourage children to design an experiment which tests the effect of changing the distance between the fulcrum, load and effort. Record and analyse your results.

Further information

Amazing Science: Forces and Motion by Sally Hewitt
(Wayland, 2007)

Simple Machines: Levers by Chris Oxlade
(Franklin Watts, 2007)

Scoop, Seesaw and Raise: A Book About Levers by
Michael Dahl and Denise Shea
(Picture Window Books, 2002)

Very Useful Machines: Levers by Chris Oxlade
(Heinemann, 2004)

Adult Reference

The Way Things Work by David Macaulay
and Neil Ardley (Dorling Kindersley, 2004)

Index

arms 24

body 24

bones 24

elbow joint 24

energy 6

force 6, 7

force arm 12

fulcrum 12, 17, 19 21, 22, 24

load arm 12

machines 4, 5 24, 26

muscles 24

nutcracker 22

pulling 6, 7

pushing 6, 7

seesaw 16, 18

shape 20

size 20

Stone Age 9

tongs 23

weight 16, 18, 19,

wheelbarrow 21